Meet the Gang

You can read more stories about the gang from Buffin Street by collecting the rest of the series.

For complete list, look at the back of the book.

Meet the Gang

Francesca Simon

Illustrated by Emily Bolam

Orion
Children's Books

Meet the Gang first appeared in *Miaow Miaow Bow Wow*
first published in Great Britain in 2000
by Orion Children's Books
This edition first published in Great Britain in 2011
by Orion Children's Books
a division of the Orion Publishing Group Ltd
Orion House
5 Upper St Martin's Lane
London WC2H 9EA
An Hachette UK Company

1 3 5 7 9 10 8 6 4 2

A catalogue record for this book is available from the British Library.

ISBN 978 1 4440 0199 0

Printed in China

The Orion Publishing Group's policy is to use papers that are natural,
renewable and recyclable products made from wood grown in sustainable forests.
The logging and manufacturing processes are expected to conform
to the environmental regulations of the country of origin.

www.orionbooks.co.uk

Hello from everyone

Woof

Honey

Miaow

Millie

on Buffin Street

Flick

Prince

Miaow

Lola

Snuffle
snuffle

Lily

Caw Caw

Do-Re-Mi

Rustle
rustle

Jogger

Growl

Sour Puss

Miaow

Joey

Bow wow

Dizzy

Miaow

Kit

Squeak Squeak

Doris Boris

Fang

Woof

Welcome to Buffin Street!

Come and join all the Buffin Street dogs, cats, rabbits, puppies and parrots, and find out what *really* goes on when their people are out of sight…

"New kid on the block!
New kid on the block!
Everyone meet up at Fang's!"

Do-Re-Mi the parrot squawked the
news up and down Buffin Street.

She flew from Prince's garden
to Fang's patio…

…and all the way up to Millie's
catflap on the third floor.

She circled across the alley and even shouted the news through Moby Dick's window.

Prince the poodle stopped
admiring his new blue ribbons.

Sour Puss stopped eyeing
Jogger the hamster as
he ran in his wheel.

Lola lifted her head from
her red velvet cushion with
the gold tassles and yawned.

Kit, Joey and Flick stopped
yowling at each other on
the alley wall.

Even Dizzy stopped
chasing his tail.

"Who is it?" Dizzy asked.

Do-Re-Mi fluffed her feathers.
"A little golden puppy,"
said Do-Re-Mi.

"Great," said Dizzy.
His droopy ears perked up.
"That means...
lots of chasing!"

"Just as long as she keeps well
away from my garden," said Prince.
"I don't want any mess."
"Where's she living?" asked Dizzy.

"At Fang's," said Do-Re-Mi.
"Let's go!"

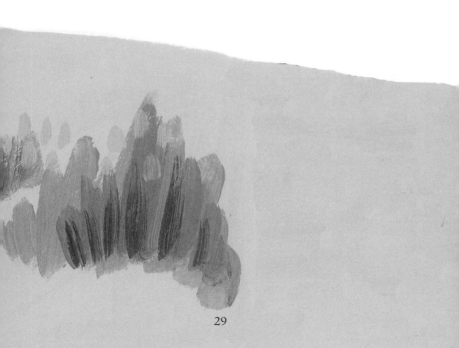

They all dashed to Fang's place
to meet the newcomer.

Prince, his lovely diamond
collars sparkling in the sun,
ambled down to the gate
between his house and Fang's.

Lily the floppy-eared rabbit
burrowed out of her hutch
through her secret tunnel,
followed by her baby bunnies.

The alley cats Kit, Joey and
Flick wriggled underneath
the broken fence.

Dizzy pushed through
his dog-flap and thumped
down the fire escape.

36

Lola gazed down like a queen
from her second floor balcony.

Fang met them all at the gate.
He did not look very pleased.

"I suppose you've come
to see her," he said.

"Though why my people want
another dog when they've
got me is a mystery."

"What's she like?" asked
Sour Puss, scowling.

"Noisy?

Dirty?

Excitable?"

Honey bounced out.
"Hi, everybody!" she barked.
"I'm Honey!"

"Noisy, just as I thought,"
grumbled Sour Puss.

She stalked off.

"Don't mind Sour Puss,
she's always a bit crabby,"
said Do-Re-Mi.
"Welcome to Buffin Street,
Honey."

"This might look like an
ordinary, every day sort of street,
but it's a very special one.
Come and see the sights!"

"My garden's next door,"
said Prince. "Keep out!
And no jumping on me
with muddy paws."

"Oh," said Honey.
Her tail stopped wagging.

"There's lots to do at my place,"
said Lily, her long ears dangling
almost to the ground.

"We've got stepping stones
to hop on and loads of
flowers to nibble."

"Best digging is at the empty
house next door to Prince's,"
said Dizzy. "I've buried lots
of good bones there…

...And wait till you roll in the
squishy mud by Foxham Pond!
There are ducks to chase,
and squirrels too!"

"Great!" said Honey.

"Best bins are at Bert's Beanery,"
said Joey.

"You would not believe the delicious
things he throws away! Burnt toast,
sour milk, and fish heads!"

"Maybe you can join our gang,"
said Kit.

"When you're older,"
said Flick.

"Thanks!" said Honey.
She thought she'd quite like
to be in a gang.

"What's it called?"

"The Wild Ones!" said Kit.

"The Outlaws!" said Joey.

"The Lizards Gizzards!" said Flick.

"We're still deciding,"
said Kit.

"Best climbing trees are in front
of Do-Re-Mi and Lily's home,"
said Millie.

"I'm not a very good climber,"
said Honey.

"And here's the secret hole
in the broken fence," said Lily.
"Perfect for sneaking out and about."

"No one knows more about escaping than Lily," said Millie. "I hope you'll come up and visit me sometime, Honey, though I do live up a lot of stairs."

"How many?"
asked Honey.

She didn't like climbing
lots of stairs.

Millie shrugged.
"More than I can count.
But if you come you can meet
my friends Doris and Boris.
They're the mice who live with me."

Honey's eyes opened wide.
"You're friends with ... mice?"

"Sure," said Millie.
"What's the big deal?"

Fang looked up from
where he'd been hiding his
head between his paws.

"Just leave me alone,"
he muttered.
"And don't touch my bones."

"Fang!" said Do-Re-Mi.
"That's not very kind."

"I don't care," said Fang.
"My life is ruined."

Honey bounced up to Fang.
"You won't be sorry I've come,
Fang!" she barked. "Promise!"

"Huh," muttered Fang.

"That's all of us," said Do-Re-Mi.
"We meet every Monday morning
at your house, and every Friday
afternoon in Foxham Park."

"How do you all get out?"
asked Honey.

"We have our ways,"
said Do-Re-Mi softly.
"There's a loose board in the fence
between your house and mine.
Dizzy has a dog flap his person
always forgets to close. And Prince
knows how to unlatch his back door."

"Wow," said Honey.
This was certainly no
ordinary place.

"Welcome to Buffin Street!"
said Do-Re-Mi.

Woof
follow me

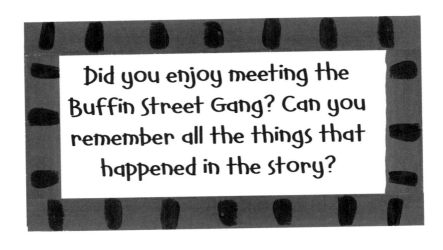

Did you enjoy meeting the Buffin Street Gang? Can you remember all the things that happened in the story?

Who tells everyone about the new arrival to Buffin Street?

Where does Honey live?

What kind of animal is Lily?

What does Sour Puss
think about Honey?

Where is the best digging
in Buffin Street?

Where are the best bins in Buffin Street?

What are the names
of Millie's mice
friends?

Where do the Buffin Street Gang meet?

For more adventures with the
Buffin Street Gang, look out for
the other books in the series.

Yum Yum

Rampage
in Prince's
Garden

Jogger's Big Adventure

Miaow Miaow Bow Wow

The Haunted House of Buffin Street

Look at Me